Ingrid Jacobson Clarfield's

Artistic Preparation and Performance Ser...

Moonlight Sonata

1st Movement
Op. 27, No. 2

by Ludwig van Beethoven

With heartfelt thanks and sincere appreciation to the following people who helped me in preparing this book:
Dean Elder, Amy Hoffman, E. L. Lancaster, Kim Newman, and Kelly Setler.

This book is dedicated to my wonderful husband, Mel Mack, whose support and encouragement I cherish.

 Foreword

Artistic performance begins with artistic preparation. The purpose of this series is to guide you through the three learning stages that lead to an artistic performance.

STAGE ONE

Preparatory and Introductory Practice . . . 3

Before the first version of the music, *Preparation and Practice Score,* you will find background information about the piece *(Introduction)* as well as helpful hints to write in the score which will simplify accurate learning *(Pencil Points)*. This first stage of learning includes *Preparatory Exercises* and *Practice Suggestions* that will prepare you for the technical and musical concepts in the music.

Some *Musical Considerations* follow, with suggestions for articulation, dynamics and pedaling. From this beginning stage of learning, always practice with these interpretive ideas in mind.

STAGE TWO

Creative and Efficient Practice 12

Once you have learned to play the piece comfortably at a slow tempo, proceed to the next section, entitled *Creative and Efficient Practice.* Practice suggestions are given to improve technical and musical aspects as you gradually increase the tempo. A variety of practice techniques are discussed in the text and analyzed in the *Preparation and Practice Score.*

Preparation and Practice Score 14

STAGE THREE

Polishing for an Artistic Performance . . . 18

The final learning stage is polishing for performance. This section gives detailed performance instructions, many of which are written in the *Artistic Performance Score.* Ideas on articulation, dynamics and pedaling are given, as well as suggestions for performance choreography, tempo, phrasing and rubato. Lyrics are provided to help capture the moods of the music and assist you in conveying your artistry to the audience. Fingering is not included to facilitate reading of the artistic ideas. Feel free to add finger numbers that are essential for solidifying the performance.

Take the necessary time to proceed through each stage of practice. The road to artistic performance is paved with conscientious technical and musical preparation.

Artistic Performance Score 20

Stage One: *Preparatory and Introductory Practice*

Use with *Preparation and Practice Score* (page 14).

INTRODUCTION: About the Music

The first movement of Ludwig van Beethoven's (1770–1827) Sonata Op. 27, No. 2 is the most famous movement among his thirty-two sonatas. The title, "Moonlight Sonata," was assigned to it by a publisher who borrowed it from an article by Heinrich Rellstab. Rellstab claimed the music was inspired by the vision "of a boat on Lake Lucerne by a luminous light." While this is a wonderful image for this piece, Beethoven had never visited Lake Lucerne. In Beethoven's time, it was nicknamed the "Laube" (Arbor) Sonata, because it was believed he composed it in an arbor. Carl Czerny, in his *On the Proper Performance of All Beethoven's Works for the Piano*, wrote: "It is a night scene in which the voice of a complaining spirit is heard at a distance."

The exact title is "Sonata quasi una Fantasia," (Sonata in the style of a Fantasy). By giving it this title, Beethoven seems to be justifying his desire to break the rules of composition in the classical period. This is demonstrated by his avoidance of the typical sonata-allegro form for the first movement. While there are elements similar to this traditional classical form, it seems more like an improvisation in a three-part form.

Beethoven composed Sonata Op. 27, No. 2 in 1802, a significant period in his life. In letters he confessed his love for one of his students, Countess Giuletta Guicciardi, who was from an aristocratic family. She was considered by many to be his "Immortal Beloved." Her admiration for him, however, was only as a pianist and teacher. During the same year Beethoven also learned that he would eventually become completely deaf for the rest of his life. He poured out his desperation to his brothers in a famous document called "The Heiligenstadt Testament."

This background information should be useful in helping you learn and perform one of the most beautiful and famous compositions in the piano repertoire. While there are two other movements, it is acceptable to perform only one movement of a sonata. Beethoven himself recommended this to one of his students, Ferdinand Rees.

4

OVERVIEW

By carefully studying the score and marking helpful hints into the music, you will simplify the early learning stages of this piece. Careful analysis can guarantee a much more accurate reading and understanding of the musical score.

Form

This piece is in a modified ABA′ form with an Introduction and a Coda.

Pencil Points

Using the *Preparation and Practice Score* (page 14), write the following into the music:

Introduction: mm. 1–5

A: mm. 5–28

B: mm. 28–42

A′: mm. 42–60

Coda: mm. 60–69

Sectional Work

Practicing this piece in sections will make learning easier and facilitate memorization.

Pencil Points

Divide the piece into smaller learning sections by writing the following numbers in your score:

(1) mm. 1–5   (7) mm. 32–38
(2) mm. 5–9   (8) mm. 38–42
(3) mm. 10–15   (9) mm. 42–46
(4) mm. 15–23   (10) mm. 46–51
(5) mm. 23–28   (11) mm. 51–60
(6) mm. 28–31   (12) mm. 60–69

PREVIEW OF POTENTIAL PROBLEMS

Clefs and Key Changes

Pencil Points

1. Before you begin to play the piece, circle or highlight the clef changes in the *Preparation and Practice Score*. This will help to avoid potentially humorous misreadings. There are 9 clef changes.

2. Knowing what key you are in at various parts will help with memorization. Mark the following into your music:
   - m. 1:   c♯ minor
   - m. 9:   E Major
   - m. 15: b minor; B Major
   - m. 23: f♯ minor
   - m. 28: G♯ Major
   - m. 42: c♯ minor
   - m. 46: E major
   - m. 60: c♯ minor

PRACTICE SUGGESTIONS

Although this piece is rather long, several of the sections have similar technical and musical problems. Therefore, you can learn and practice these similar sections together. This technique will be referred to as *Pair Practice*. Learn the *Preparatory Exercises* first and use them as warm-ups later in your practice. This piece will probably take you several weeks to learn. Take your time to learn the music carefully so that you can observe all the details specified by the composer, plus the numerous suggestions by the editor.

Section 1 (mm. 1–5)

PREPARATORY EXERCISES

These exercises reinforce the LH octaves and the RH triplets.

A.1 LH Octaves Using Finger Substitutions

Play the LH octaves legato. If your hands are large enough, you may choose to connect the LH octaves by using a 5–4 finger substitution. For consistency, change to 4 on beat 4, except in m. 3 where you need to switch to 4 on beat 2.

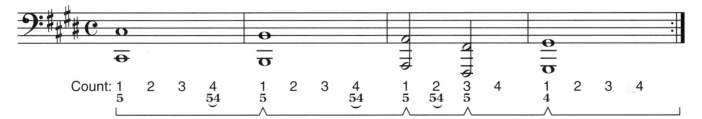

A.2 LH Octaves

If your hands are smaller, use fingers 1 and 5 on each octave and move your hand to the next octave on beat 4. In m. 3 you will move to the next octave on beats 2 and 4. If you change the pedal smoothly and clearly immediately after you shift to the next octave, it will create a good legato.

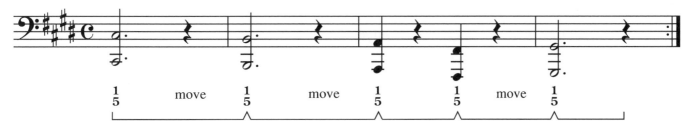

- Whether you choose exercise **A.1** or **A.2**, be sure your wrist and forearm remain relaxed on each octave, and listen for a soft but sustained sound.

- Listen for a clear change of pedal immediately after you play beat 1 of mm. 1, 2 and 4 and after beats 1 and 3 of m. 3.

B. RH Triplets

This exercise prepares the circular wrist motion needed to play the legato triplets that recur throughout the piece.

- Keep your fingers close to the keys and use small circular wrist motions to create soft flowing triplets.

- Listen carefully that each note is even and smoothly connected.

---

mm. 1–5

1. Practice the RH alone blocking each chord. To "block" means to simultaneously play all the notes that form a pattern. This is indicated in the score by BL . Pay attention to the suggested fingering to facilitate a good legato, when you play the notes of each triplet individually as written.

2. Practice the LH alone, choosing one of the two fingerings suggested in *Preparatory Exercise* A.1 or A.2.

3. Practice HT, playing soft blocked chords in the RH.

Section 2 (mm. 5–9)

PREPARATORY EXERCISES

These exercises prepare the RH fifth-finger melody in the first theme. The top note must sing out clearly above the soft triplet accompaniment.

A.1 Singing Melody over Soft Triplets

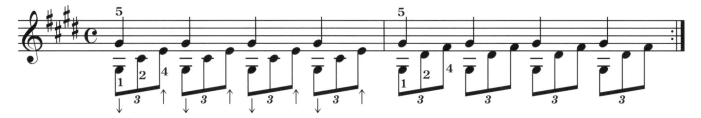

- Use a small down (↓) up (↑) wrist motion on each of the triplets.

- Keep a good arched position on your fifth finger, and play on the fingertip. This will help create a clear sound.

- The top note should sing out while the triplets remain soft and even.

A.2 Singing Melody over Soft Triplets

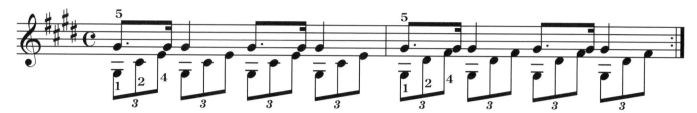

- Make sure the ♪ sounds exactly midway between the third note of the triplet and the following quarter note. Maintain a loose wrist to assist in keeping the ♪ light and elegant, and be sure it connects to the ♩.

- Listen for smooth soft triplets under a singing top note melody. All the top notes should be equal in tone.

mm. 5–9

1. Practice the RH alone. If your hands are large enough, block each chord. Then play the RH alone slowly as written. If you cannot reach the interval of a ninth in m. 8 (A to B), try the suggested redistribution ⓑ, that suggests playing the A with your LH. This will allow the top note to sing out easily.

2. Practice the LH alone with pedal. Either use the suggested finger substitutions in the score, or move your hand as recommended in Section 1,

Preparatory Exercise A.2. In mm. 5 and 6, note that the LH outer notes move down a half step, but the middle notes remain the same.

3. Practice HT with the metronome at ♪ = 60–80 (one tick per triplet eighth note) so you can be sure to keep each eighth note of the triplets even. The ♪, as in m. 5, also needs to be very even. Make sure it forms a "musical unit" with the half note that follows. Always listen for a clear beautiful melody.

Section 3 (mm. 10–15)

PREPARATORY EXERCISE

A. LH Octaves

This exercise prepares the LH legato octaves.

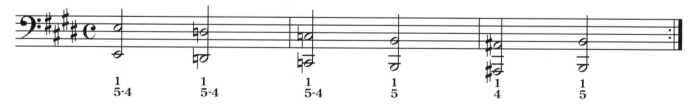

- To move from a white key to a black key, use 5 on the B and 4 on the A♯.

- Always keep your wrist and forearm loose and fingertips firm. Your thumb should move down gently, but cannot be truly legato.

mm. 10–15

1. Practice the RH alone. If your hands are large enough, block each chord. Then play the RH alone slowly as written. Always listen for a clear melody above the soft, even triplets.

2. Practice the LH alone with pedal. Follow the finger substitutions if your hands are large enough.

3. Practice HT with metronome at ♪ =60–80.

Section 4 (mm. 15–23)

PREPARATORY EXERCISES

A. LH octaves using 2nd Finger as a Pivot

This exercise prepares using the 2nd finger as a pivot
to connect B to E in mm. 16 and 18, and F♯ to B in
mm. 20–21.

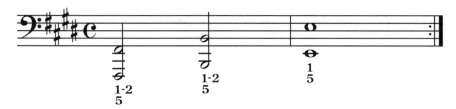

- Use the suggested 1–2 fingering substitution, so that you can smoothly connect the octaves. By using the second finger as a pivot (on F♯, then B), you can also connect the octaves without looking at your hands.

- Keep your wrist and forearm loose, and your fingertips firm.

- Change the pedal immediately after you switch to the next octave.

mm. 15–23

Learn this section using the Practice Suggestions for
Section 2.

Section 5 (mm. 23–28)

PREPARATORY EXERCISE

A. Chord Inversions

This exercise prepares the legato broken chord inversion in m. 23.

- Try both suggested fingerings and choose the one that is more comfortable for your hand.

- Make a small circular motion with your wrist for each broken chord.

- Listen for a smooth, even, legato sound.

mm. 23–28

1. Practice this section RH alone, blocking each chord first. Remember to keep your wrist loose when you block, to avoid forearm tension.

2. Practice the LH alone. If your hands are big enough, try the suggested finger substitutions.

3. Practice HT with metronome at ♪=60–80.

Section 6 (mm. 28–31)

PREPARATORY EXERCISE

A. Top Note Melody within a Broken Chord

This exercise will reinforce bringing out the melody
notes in mm. 28 and 30.

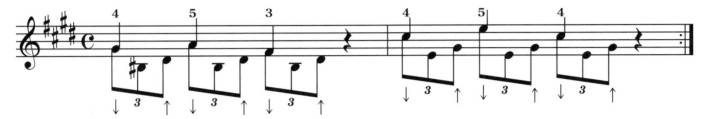

- Drop the wrist slightly on each ♩ to give extra arm weight. This will help you bring out the melody.

- The wrist should come up gently on the second and third notes of each triplet.

---

mm. 28–31

Pencil Points

1. Circle or highlight the double stemmed notes to remind you that they are melody notes.

2. Practice the RH alone blocking each chord. In m. 30 block the octave on beat one. After you feel comfortable blocking, play as written.

Listen for a clear melody note while keeping the accompaniment softer than the melody.

3. If your hands are small, use the alternate fingering in m. 29.

Section 7 (mm. 32–38)

This section is often the trickiest for many students.
The key to successful learning is finding a fingering
that works for you. The editor has suggested two
fingerings. Practice the following exercises and then
decide which fingering you prefer.

A. RH Blocked Chords using Fingering #1

- If your hands are large enough, play all notes together to reinforce the pattern.

- Sink into the keys with a loose wrist and forearm.

B. RH Blocked Intervals Using Fingering #1 and #2

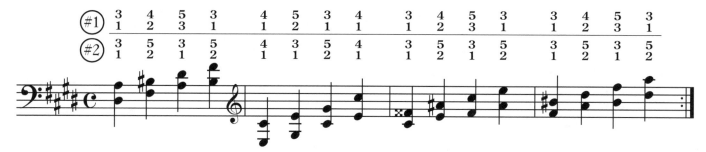

For smaller hands, play the RH broken chords in two–note blocked intervals to reinforce the pattern.

Pencil Points

1. Write in extra accidentals to help you remember them: (e.g. m. 34 – F⊗ & A♯, m. 35 – B♯ & A♮, m. 36 – B♯, m. 37 – B♯).

2. In m. 37, circle or highlight the D♯ and C♯ on beats 3 and 4 to remember to hold them and bring them out.

mm. 32–38

1. Practice the RH alone, trying all three suggested fingerings. Listen for a smooth, even sound on every note. Helpful hint: In m. 32, all the notes are sharped except A. Don't forget that B♯ is a white key (C♮). In m. 34, all the notes are sharped, but E♯ and F⊗ are white keys. (F♮ and G♮).

2. Practice very slowly, focusing on how your wrist moves sideways to maneuver around the black- and white-key combinations. Try as much as possible to keep your eyes on the music, and really feel the intervals.

Section 8 (mm. 38–42)

PREPARATORY EXERCISE

A. RH Lower Note Melody Within a Broken Chord

This exercise will reinforce bringing out the melody when it is the lower note within a broken-chord pattern. With a loose wrist, sink into each melody note with a downward wrist motion (↓). Let the wrist go up (⌣↗) on the second two notes of each triplet.

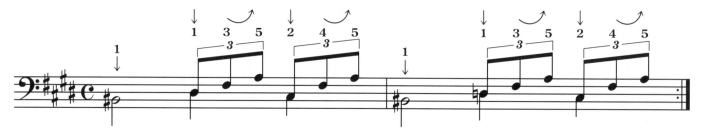

Pencil Points

Circle the B♯s in mm. 38–40 and write "hold" beside each.

mm. 38–42

1. Practice RH alone, blocking each chord to reinforce the pattern.

2. Practice LH alone, trying the finger substitutions if your hands are large enough.

Section 9 (mm. 42–46)

Follow *Preparatory Exercises* and Practice Suggestions for Section 2.

Section 10 (mm. 46–51)

The *Preparatory Exercises* for Section 1–4 will have prepared you for the technical requirements for this section.
Follow the Practice Suggestions for Section 3.

Pencil Points

To assist you later in memorizing, compare m. 9 with m. 46 and notice the changes. In m. 47, circle the D♯ in the LH and write in the sharp to remind you not to go to D♮ this time.

Section 11 (mm. 51–60)

Follow the Practice Suggestions for Section 4. If your hands are small, try the alternate fingering in footnote ⓑ on page 14. Take the lower note of each ninth in mm. 52, 54, and 59 with the LH.

Section 12 (mm. 60–69)

PREPARATORY EXERCISE

A. RH Blocked Intervals

This exercise prepares the shifting hand position to play m. 64 legato.

- With a loose wrist, move sideways freely to facilitate moving in and out of the white and black keys. Play inside on the white, and move out on the black keys.

- Try both fingerings and select the one that is more comfortable.

B. RH Blocked Intervals using Hand Contraction

This exercise prepares the contraction of the hand needed to play m. 65 legato.

- Follow the fingering carefully, keeping your eyes on the music so you can really feel the intervals as your hand contracts.

- Keep your wrist moving sideways freely.

Pencil Points:

1. Cross out the tied notes in mm. 63 and 65.
2. Circle the B♯ in mm. 63 and 65, and write "hold" beside each.

USING THE METRONOME

To be sure the triplets are even, some metronome practice will be useful during the early stages of learning this piece. Begin your practice with the metronome at ♪=60–80 and gradually increase to ♪=120 or 𝅘𝅥𝅮𝅘𝅥𝅮𝅘𝅥𝅮 or ♩=40.

MUSICAL CONSIDERATIONS

Touch

The *Preparatory Exercises* will prepare you for the continuous legato required for this piece. For the first stages of learning, as you practice under tempo, listen for smooth, even triplets. To achieve this legato, feel the weight transfer from each finger to the next while you keep your wrist and forearm loose. The upper-note melody will sing out if you keep your fingertips firm and your wrist loose. Sink into the keys on each LH octave, keeping your forearm loose.

Dynamics/Balance

Bringing out the melody with a beautiful singing tone is the most important element of a successful performance of this piece. Usually the melody is in the top voice, which will require extra arm weight on that note, while keeping the wrist loose. Notice where the melody is not on the top (mm. 29, 37–40). The supporting bass note must always be soft, but have a rich tone. The triplets must always flow softly in the background. Pay attention to Beethoven's dynamic markings, plus the editorial suggestions marked in gray.

Pedal

First practice without pedal, so that you can achieve as clear a legato as possible with your fingers. Beethoven specifically expected the performer to use the pedal with his direction "senza sordino." This translates to "without mutes," which indicates to raise the dampers, or use the pedal. However, he was not specific as to where to change the pedal. One clearly needs to change the pedal with each bass note. All pedal markings in this edition are editorial.

 # Stage Two: *Creative and Efficient Practice*

Use with *Preparation and Practice Score* (page 14).

This next stage of practice should begin only AFTER the *Preparatory and Introductory Practice* section has been successfully completed. The successful completion of one stage lays the groundwork for the next. Both of these stages will lead to *Stage Three: Polishing for an Artistic Performance.*

EFFICIENT PRACTICE

Because there are so many potential technical problems that recur in various sections of this piece, it is very important that you organize and maximize your practice time by being very efficient in working on these passages. Below are different ways to practice, focusing on the specific problem according to WHERE it is and WHAT it is. Always begin your practice with the most difficult measures.

Since this piece is in a modified ABA' form, themes repeat. Therefore, sections can be *Pair Practiced*. To *Pair Practice* is to practice similar sections one after the other. This is a useful practice technique that allows you to tackle similar technical and musical concerns and will also facilitate memorization.

Throughout your practice, pay careful attention to Beethoven's original dynamic markings, as well as additional ones provided by the editor in gray. Feel free to experiment with your own ideas. A rule for proper balance is to keep the bass line one dynamic level below the melody, and the triplets two levels below. For example, if the melody is *mp*, the bass should be *p* and the triplets *pp*.

Observe all pedaling suggestions as well, but be sure to sometimes practice without pedal. At all times focus on a clear melody with a soft, smooth, and even triplet accompaniment.

Section 1 (mm. 1–5)

1. Practice HT, "blocking" all three notes in the RH to solidify the feel of each broken chord.

2. Play as written, listening for a smooth even legato on every note in the RH. In the LH, remember to prepare the next octave by moving, or using a finger substitution.

Section 2 (mm. 5–9)

Pair Practice with Sections 3, 5, 9, 10

1. Practice the top note of the RH together with the LH. Listen for a beautiful singing melody, and a solid bass.

2. Now practice the RH part with "two for one" technique. This is indicated in the score by ②₄.

   A. Play the treble staff notes using two hands—

the top notes with the RH and the lower notes with the LH. Using this technique, you can more easily play the top note louder for appropriate balance.

   B. Now play as written with the RH alone. Listen for the same balance you achieved while playing with two hands.

3. Practice HT, always listening for a clear top-note melody, solid but softer bass, and soft even triplets. Be sure the ♪ in mm. 5 and 6 is gentle and comes after the third note of the triplet; it should form a "musical unit" with the following note.

Section 3 (mm. 10–15)

Follow the Practice Suggestions for Section 2.

mm. 12 and 13
1. Play the LH octaves a little louder and shape them, since they are a counter-melody.
2. Listen for a clear pedal change on each octave.

Section 4 (mm. 15–23)

Pair Practice with Section 11.

mm. 15–18
1. Practice the top note of the RH together with the LH.
2. Practice the RH part using ②₄ technique. Listen for a clear top-note melody. (See Section 2, No. 2.)
3. Practice RH alone, or use the redistribution suggested in the Practice Suggestions for Section 2, No. 1 on page 7.
4. Practice LH alone listening for beautifully connected octaves. If you take the redistribution ⓑ make sure that the B in the LH is soft and unaccented.
5. Practice HT always listening for a clear top note melody and legato octaves in the bass.
6. In m. 15, be sure to change the pedal on beat 3, when it changes from b minor to B Major.

Section 5 (mm. 23–28)

Pair Practice with Section 2.

1. Practice RH alone beginning with m. 22, beat 3, to help determine which fingering is more comfortable in m. 23.
2. Follow the Practice Suggestions for Section 2.
3. Observe Beethoven's crescendo and diminuendo markings in mm. 25 and 27.

Section 6 (mm. 28–31)

1. Practice RH alone "blocking."
2. Practice RH part using (2/1) technique. In mm. 28 and 30 play the melody notes with the RH, and in mm. 29 and 31 play the melody note with the LH.
3. Play RH alone imitating the proper balance you achieved using both hands.
4. Play HT following the suggested pedaling which will help make the melody come out clearly.

Section 7 (mm. 32–38)

1. Review the Preparatory Exercises for this section every day to solidify the pattern and finalize your fingering choice.
2. To drill the leap from the end of m. 32 to m. 33, practice the grouping marked "1" until you are confident. Then play Group 2, followed by Group 1, (2 + 1). Finally, play all three groups (2 + 1 + 3). Use this practice technique when you have difficulty in the MIDDLE of a passage. This is called "Add-A-Group" and is abbreviated (AAG). The middle group will then get the extra practice required to facilitate an easier transition.
3. Use (AAG) for mm. 34 and 35.
4. In mm. 36 and 37 block each set of two notes with your choice of fingering. To solidify the feel of the different intervals and fingering, play each set of two notes four times, (as you would play a trill). Continue trilling each set of 2 notes three times, then two times, and finally play as written. This is called "Trilling 4 to 1" and is abbreviated (TR4→1). This technique is helpful in strengthening weaker fingers and solidifying broken intervals.

Section 8 (mm. 38–42)

1. Practice RH alone "blocking."
2. Practice the RH part using (2/1) technique.
3. Practice LH m. 40 to the downbeat of m. 42 without pedal, keeping your arm loose and listening for good legato octaves.
4. Practice HT listening for a clear alto melody and legato octaves.

Section 9 (mm. 42–46)

Pair Practice with Section 2.

1. Since this section is identical to Section 2, follow all the practice instructions for Section 2.
2. To facilitate memorization, also *pair practice* the transitions into sections 3 and 10 by practicing mm. 9 through 11 and mm. 46 and 47. Notice the differences as you play.

Section 10 (mm. 46–51)

Pair Practice with Section 2.

mm. 48–49
Observe Beethoven's crescendo in m. 48. To highlight the *p*, be sure to lift the hand and not connect the C♯ at the end of m. 48 to the D♯ on the downbeat of m. 49.

Section 11 (mm. 51–60)

Pair Practice with Section 4.

mm. 51–55
1. Notice that this is a transposition of mm. 15–18. *Pair Practice* both sets of measures.

Pencil Points

1. To assist in memorization write in m. 51, c♯ minor on beat 1, C♯ Major on beat 3, and in m. 24, C♯ Major.
2. In m. 56 write "changes," since here the pattern is altered from what it was in Section 4. Compare mm. 18–23 with mm. 54–60.

mm. 56–58
1. Practice the soprano and bass alone to hear the duet between the voices.
2. Practice the RH using (2/1) technique.
3. Practice HT listening for good balance between melody and accompaniment.

mm. 59–60
Pair Practice with mm. 8–9.

Section 12 (mm. 60–69)

1. Practice the LH part using (2/1) technique. The upper note should be a little louder than the lower note, since it is the melody.
2. Practice the LH alone, listening for good balance.
3. After doing the practice suggestions listed below, practice the entire section HT. Listen for good balance.

mm. 60, 61, and 66
1. Practice the RH alone blocking each chord.
2. Play the RH alone listening for smooth even triplets.

mm. 62–65
1. Practice the RH alone blocking each set of two-note intervals.
2. Use (TR4→1) (see Section 7, No. 4).
3. Practice HT. Listen for good balance and bring out both the LH melody and the ♩ B♯ in mm. 63 and 65.

PRACTICE TEMPOS

Only minimal practice time should be done with the metronome. Your focus needs to be more on sound and balance than on a strict tempo. Occasionally check that your triplets are even by setting the metronome from ♪=80 to ♪=120. To assist you in gradually increasing the tempo and attaining a more flowing feeling, practice with the metronome at ♩=40 and gradually increase to ♩=50.

Sonata Quasi Una Fantasia

Preparation and Practice Score

1st Movement

Ludwig van Beethoven
(1770–1827)
Op. 27, No. 2

(a) For a true legato, if possible switch from 5 to 4 to connect to the next octave (see Preparatory Exercise 1, page 7).

(b) For smaller hands, play the bracketed note with the left hand.

ⓒ Lift pedal halfway if using alternate fingering ⓑ.

Stage Three: *Polishing for an Artistic Performance*

Use with *Artistic Performance Score* (page 20).

Achieving an artistic performance of this piece is easy if you have observed Beethoven's dynamics markings, solidified your fingering, and listened for good balance in the first two stages of practice. To create the proper mood for the audience, you will need to be physically involved, but in a calm and understated manner. Dynamics will also need to be subtle. Go back to page 3 and read "About the Music" to refresh your memory about suggested imagery in this composition. Strive to find your own image that will help you create the desired mood.

THE GRAND ENTRANCE

This piece needs a serene and tranquil opening. Begin with your head down and your hands in your lap. In your head create a picture that will help you feel the calmness and solemnity, and therefore assist the audience in experiencing the desired tranquility. Slowly lift your head and hands, as you gently prepare your feet on both pedals. With both hands on the keyboard, hear one measure in your head before beginning. Then gently lift your wrists and breathe before playing the first note.

PERFORMANCE CONSIDERATIONS

Body Language and Choreography

To portray the calm deep feeling required in this music it is essential that you convey that with your body language. Too much physical involvement is distracting. Sitting up straight and tall does not help to convey the appropriate mood either. You will notice in the *Artistic Performance Score* several suggestions for places to lean in or to let your body move more with the melodic line.

Introduction (mm. 1–5)

Play this section with your head bowed to convey the solemn feeling needed. Lean in slightly on the downbeat of m. 5. Gracefully lift your wrists a bit to show the end of the section.

Section A (mm. 5 – 28)

While you should continue sitting quite still during this section, allow your body to lean more to show

points of intensity. In mm. 12, 16, and 18, let your body follow the direction of the LH. At the end of m. 22, gracefully lift your wrists and lean in on m. 23 to show the end of the phrase. In m. 27, sit up straight to show the highpoint of the crescendo.

Section B (mm. 28–42)

In mm. 28 to 31, lean in slightly on beat 3, so your body conveys the feeling of $\texttt{<}\quad\texttt{>}$. Allow your body to flow gently to the right as you move up the keyboard in mm. 32–35. As you end each measure, make a graceful arc-like gesture with your arm. Let your body lean to the left to begin the next measure.

In mm. 37 to 39, lean in to show the intensity of the D♯, C♯, B♯ melody. Once again, lift your wrist and lean in at the end of the section.

Section A´ (mm. 42–60)

Follow the choreography suggestions for Section A.

Coda (mm. 60–68)

As you did in the B section, let your body follow the ascending and descending triplets in mm. 62–66. Allow your head to drop on the low C♯ in m. 68.

Dynamics/Balance

Beethoven has been very specific about his dynamics: "si deve suonare tutto questo pezzo delicatissimamente e senza sordino," which means: "this entire piece must be played very delicately and without dampers (with pedal)." He also writes in "sempre pianissimo e senza sordino." He is reminding us to play "always very softly and without dampers." Within all this soft playing, there still need to be gradations of volume. Follow Beethoven's dynamics as well as the additional ones provided by the editor. Observe the tenuto marks (—) (in mm. 1, 4, 16, 18, 22, 23, 41, 52, 54, and 57) that suggest slightly more emphasis on these notes. Stress these notes to highlight the dissonance. They should sound like a cry of anguish. Sometimes notes have also been circled to show they are more important and need to be brought out slightly. (See mm. 4, 12, 37–40, 63–66). Feel free to experiment with your own ideas that will still maintain the desired mood. With the proper technical preparation and efficient practice strategies you have used so far, the proper balance of melody and accompaniment should be easy to attain. Notice the additional editorial dynamic markings throughout the piece to help vary the level of intensity of the melody.

Shaping/Phrasing

This piece contains primarily four–measure phrases. The shaping of each phrase should be very subtle to maintain the appropriate mood. Beethoven has written in some very specific shaping ⟨ ⟩ in mm. 16, 18, 28–31, 52, 54 and 62–65. Follow these carefully, experimenting with varying the levels of intensity. Notice the additional editorial dynamic markings for shaping long phrases that will help to achieve a long beautiful melodic line. These are indicated in the Artistic Performance Score. The short slurs added in m. 57 (including pickup) will help to highlight this measure, that is different from any other measure in the piece. Singing the melody in your head will also help you come up with your own ideas on shaping and phrasing. The lyrics provided in mm. 5–23, 28–31, and 37–40 will assist you in shaping the melody and bringing out the expressive quality and moods of the music. For those who prefer more nature-oriented words, feel free to think of the following lyrics for mm. 5–15:

See the moon   on the lake how bright - ly it   glows.

See the stars in the sky   how love - ly they shine to - night.

Tempo

To portray the calm mood required for this piece, a suggested performance tempo is ♩=50–56. The tempo must remain steady, but it is also appropriate to slow down at the end of sections. The editor has indicated this on the music with the sign 〰〰 . (See mm. 9, 14, 22, and 59). Other appropriate places to slow down are during interesting harmony changes, as in mm. 9–10, or in places you wish to highlight (e.g., the end of m. 35 to m. 36, and the end of m. 37 to m. 38). Additionally, take a little time at the end of m. 32 to m. 33, and at the end of m. 34 to m. 35 to bring out the essential improvisatory character of this section. A slight pushing-ahead of the tempo is acceptable in mm. 32–35 as it builds to the high point. Do not make a big ritard at the end (mm. 67–69). Beethoven has built one in by leaving out the triplets and writing only half notes.

Pedal

Correct pedaling techniques have been recommended throughout your early practice stages. Experiment with different levels of pedaling, and remember to adapt to the piano and the room when you perform this piece.

While Beethoven specifically wanted this piece to be soft ("sempre pianissimo"), there are definitely places that must sing out more. Try the editorial suggestions for additional places to use the *una corda* pedal marked in the Artistic Performance Score. Use the left pedal, u.c. (*una corda*), where indicated. Where it is marked t.c. (*tre corde*), lift your foot off the *una corda* pedal. Do not keep the *una corda* pedal down for the entire piece. This will keep the beautiful melody from projecting and will create a monotonous feeling. Listen carefully when you release the *una corda* pedal so the sound blends well, and is not suddenly too loud.

THE FINAL TOUCH

Maintain the mood you have created by keeping your head bowed on the last note. Hold it a few extra beats to observe the fermata. When the sound has faded away, slowly lift your hands, head, and pedal together. Let your hands float gracefully to your lap.

—————————— ✣ ——————————

Sonata Quasi Una Fantasia

Artistic Performance Score
1st Movement

Ludwig van Beethoven
(1770–1827)
Op. 27, No. 2

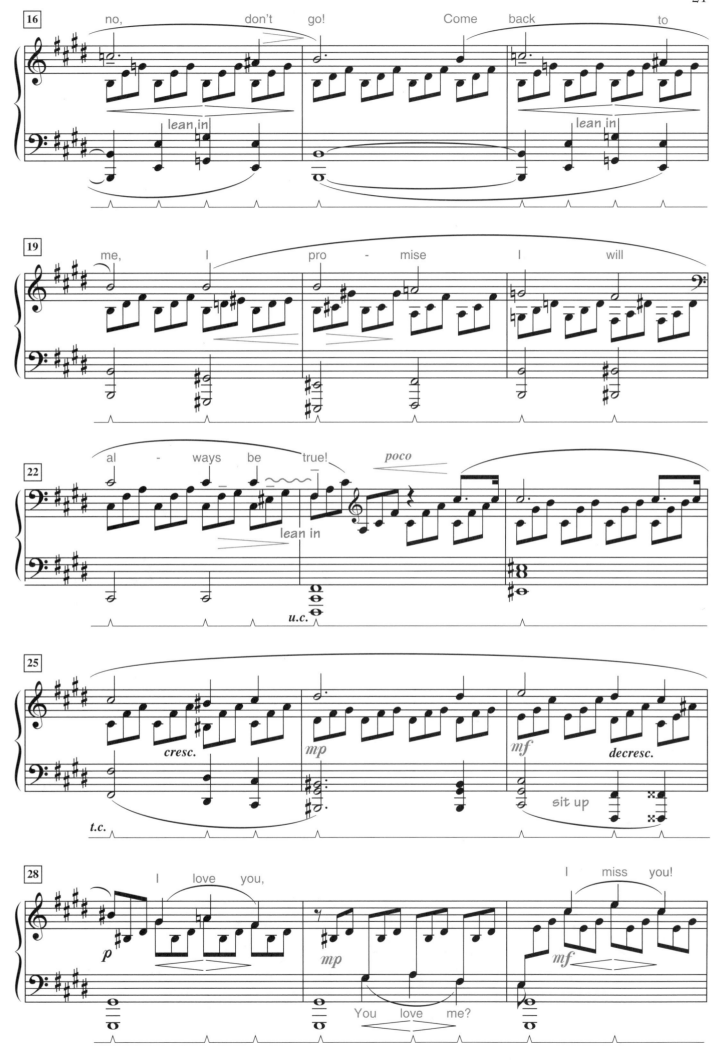

About the Author

INGRID JACOBSON CLARFIELD is nationally recognized as a teacher, clinician, author, and adjudicator. She has given lecture-recitals, workshops and master classes throughout the United States and Canada. These include teaching demonstrations at State and National Conventions of the Music Teachers National Association and national pedagogy conferences. A member of the Board of Directors of the World Piano Pedagogy Conference, Ms. Clarfield serves as Coordinator of Interactive Sessions.

Ms. Clarfield is Professor of Piano at Westminster Choir College of Rider University in Princeton, New Jersey, where since 1982, she has taught piano, piano ensemble, and courses in piano pedagogy and piano technique. In addition, she directs Westminster Choir College's Piano Week for High School Students and is guest clinician for Calgary Arts Summer School Piano Camp in Alberta, Canada.

Ms. Clarfield's pedagogical ideas are outlined in her series *From Mystery to Mastery*, Books 1 and 2, co-authored with Suzanne West Guy and published by Alfred Publishing Company. Her new edition of Debussy's *Golliwog's Cakewalk* is the first volume of her *Artistic Preparation and Performance Series*, also published by Alfred. She has written several articles that have been published in *Keyboard Companion*, *The American Music Teacher*, *Piano Life* and *Clavier*.

Ms. Clarfield maintains an independent studio in Princeton, New Jersey. Her students have performed concertos with several orchestras and have won top honors and awards in state, national, and international competitions sponsored by the MTNA, Young Keyboard Artist Association, American Music Scholarship Association, International Young Artist Piano Competition and the Steinway Society.

Since 1976, Ms. Clarfield has performed regularly in two-piano recitals with Lillian Livingston. Ms. Clarfield holds a Bachelor of Music degree from Oberlin College where she studied with John Perry, and a Master of Music degree from the Eastman School of Music.

HELPING STUDENTS SOLVE THE MYSTERY

**There is so much to learn with a new masterwork.
When master composers wrote music many years ago, they did not include a set of
instructions to prepare the student for the proper performance of a piece.
As a result, both teacher and student must work together to create their
own plan of study. *THERE IS HELP.***

From
MYSTERY TO MASTERY

A Unique and Exciting Step-by-Step Approach to Practicing and Performing
Favorite Piano Repertoire from Four Stylistic Periods

Ingrid Jacobson Clarfield and Suzanne West Guy

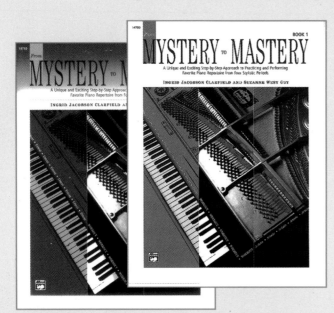

Nationally recognized teachers Ingrid Jacobson
Clarfield and Suzanne West Guy present *From
Mystery to Mastery* to share with other piano
teachers. Many of the teaching techniques
therein have resulted in outstanding students
who not only enjoy practicing, but also are
polished performers. The goal of *From Mystery to
Mastery* is to take students from their initial
encounter with the music (the Mystery) through
practicing stages to the polished performance
(the Mastery). With its unique format, students
will learn a systematic and efficient way to
prepare, analyze, practice and perform an artistic
version of the selected masterwork.

Book 1 (14709) **$12.95**
*52-page Study Guide and
44-page music insert*

• Bach *Musette in D Major*

• Clementi *Sonatina in C Major, Op. 36, No. 1*

• Schumann *Wild Rider*

• Khatchaturian *Andantino* (Ivan Sings)

Book 2 (14710) **$12.95**
*55-page Study Guide and
40-page music insert*

• Bach *Invention No. 8*

• Beethoven *Für Elise*

• Chopin *Prelude in B Minor*

• Debussy *Le Petit Nègre*

Alfred
ALFRED PUBLISHING CO., INC.
P.O. Box 10003 • 16320 Roscoe Blvd.
Van Nuys, CA 91410-0003
www.alfredpub.com

ISBN 0-7390-0805-6

0 38081 17532 4